On ~~Tour with~~
Theodore Roosevelt

The Western Presidential Campaign Trail of 1900

Filled with never before seen and unpublished photographs of
New York Governor Theodore Roosevelt and entourage

By Scott Malawski

RoseDog ❧ Books
PITTSBURGH, PENNSYLVANIA 15238

RoseDog Books
585 Alpha Drive
Suite 103
Pittsburgh, PA 15238
Visit our website at www.rosedogbookstore.com

ISBN: 979-8-88812-338-6
eISBN: 979-8-88812-838-1

Preface

This document is not intended to be another biography or historical sketch about Theodore Roosevelt, but rather a chronological photographic record of life during the western presidential campaign trail of 1900. This work is entirely composed of original, previously unpublished photographs of then New York Governor Theodore Roosevelt campaigning in Michigan, South Dakota, North Dakota, Idaho, Montana, Wyoming, and Colorado.

I purchased this collection of 44 photographs at auction in 2003 and felt these photographs were important enough to be published. I contacted Amy Verone, Chief of Cultural Affairs of Sagamore Hill Theodore Roosevelt National Historic Site, who supported my desire to publish them.

In mid-2008, I found this same collection of images and more on the Harvard University website. I now had a reference point and thus began reworking my data. Harvard's website was invaluable in helping me arrange the order of these photographs for the book, as well as providing locations which would otherwise remain unknown. The Harvard collection contains 92 images from a photo album given to the university by the Theodore Roosevelt estate in 1943. My collection of 44 photos is reproduced in this volume. Some of the photographs in my collection differ from the Harvard album. Many of my photographs have a hand-written caption on verso, which identifies the subject and location. While working with Susan Wyssen, Manuscript Cataloger at Harvard University, I discovered some discrepancies contained in my photograph inscriptions in comparison with theirs. Susan was able to verify the subject matter locations through research and utilizing a day-by-day chronology of Roosevelt's historic cross-country journey. Any differences in photograph captions are such noted in the complimenting text. The photographic order of my publication is the result of Susan's research and the photograph album in Harvard University's collection. The dates of the photographs used in my publication are guestimates loosely based on the knowledge of Roosevelt's day-to-day campaign and are printed in this volume only to give the reader a timeline of events.

The words of noted Theodore Roosevelt biographer William Roscoe Thayer echo my thoughts... "Roosevelt took his full share in campaigning for the Republican ticket. He spoke in the East and in the West, and for the first time the people of many of the States heard him speak and saw his actual presence. His attitude as a speaker, his gestures, the way in which his pent-up thoughts seemed almost to strangle him before he could utter them, his smile showing the white rows of teeth, his fist clenched as if to strike an invisible adversary, the sudden dropping of his voice, and leveling of his forefinger as he became almost conver-sational in tone, and seemed to address special individuals in the crowd before him, the strokes of sarcasm, stern and cutting, and the swift flashes of humor which set the great multitude in a roar, became in that summer and autumn familiar to millions of his countrymen; and the cartoonists made his features and gestures familiar to many other millions. Up to Election Day in November, the Republicans did not feel confident, but when the votes were counted, McKinley had a plurality of over 830,000, and beat Bryan by more than a million."

I hope you enjoy seeing these photographs and reading the captions as much as I did.

Bonus Material

Included with this publication are all the commercially produced Theodore Roosevelt recordings from Victor Talking Machine Company and Thomas Edison's National Phonograph Company from his 1912 presidential campaign. Also included are the incredibly rare 4 Berliner Gramophone Company 1898 recordings of Chief Trumpeter Emil Cassi of Roosevelt's Rough Riders demonstrating the various bugle calls used during the Spanish-American War. There are also 15 video clips of Roosevelt spanning the years 1905 – 1919.

The recordings can be found by navigating to the web address below or by scanning the QR code.

I hope these bonus items help make your Theodore Roosevelt experience an enjoyable one!

Videos https://jumpshare.com/b/iTRxiWTSuSPn7fTn1uZw
Audio   https://jumpshare.com/b/Ab0kGCB2JsBwjtYjl6T1
QR Code Video Files   QR Code Audio Files

Acknowledgements

There are many people without whose expert help and guidance, this book would not have been possible. I would like to thank Amy Verone, Chief of Cultural Affairs at Sagamore Hill Theodore Roosevelt National Historic Site for her original support and encouragement of me writing this publication. A most important thank you goes to Susan Wyssen, Manuscript Cataloger at Harvard University and Wallace Dailey, Curator of the Harvard University Theodore Roosevelt Collection who both gave me direction on my publication and answered many questions regarding their photographic collection in relation to my series of photographs.

I would also like to express gratitude to Ronnie Inda, Lisa Malawski, Robin Rolfs, Joan Rolfs, Dave Kitska, Bob Coon, brother, Barry Malawski and mother, Mildred Blutstein for their ideas, suggestions and support during my writing of this book.

Introduction

In 1896, the Republican Party nominated William McKinley for president and New Jersey Senator Garret Hobart as his vice-presidential running mate. The Democratic Party chose William Jennings Bryan as their presidential nominee, along with Arthur Sewall for vice president.

McKinley's position centered on the protective tariff and the gold standard, while Bryan favored a move towards silver to increase the nation's money supply. Bryan campaigned nationwide, conducting many whistle-stop speeches, while McKinley spoke mainly in his hometown of Canton, Ohio, partly because his wife Ida was prone to seizures and headaches, and he wanted to remain close to her.

McKinley's popularity grew as his speeches were reprinted in newspapers across the country. He won the election with more than 50% of the popular vote.

McKinley's firm stance on the protective tariff and the gold standard aided in the passing of the Dingley Tariff of 1897, resulting in an increased tariff and the passing of the Gold Standard Act of 1900.

Foreign affairs also occupied a large portion of McKinley's presidency. In 1898, Cuba was fighting for its independence from Spain. McKinley had sent the USS battleship Maine to Havana, Cuba to protect American interests. However, on February 15, 1898, the battleship Maine exploded in Havana Harbor. This event angered the United States, leading Congress to declare war on Spain in April 1898.

Theodore Roosevelt, then Assistant Secretary of the Navy, quit his post and eagerly went to Cuba with his volunteer cavalry, known as the "Rough Riders." They won the key battle at Kettle Hill (also known as San Juan Hill) on July 1, 1898, thus ending the war with Spain.

As a result, the United States added Puerto Rico and Guam as possessions and annexed the Philippines as a territory for $20 million. These new acquisitions involved the United States in Asian politics. McKinley's administration set an "Open Door Policy" regarding trade relations with China. However, by 1900, a group of Chinese nationalists known as the Boxers showed their objection to foreign intrusion by massacring western missionaries and Chinese Christians. President McKinley sent troops to aid England, Germany, Japan, Russia, and other countries, thus helping end the "Boxer Rebellion."

In 1899, Vice President Hobart died in office. Upon recommendation from Senator Tom Platt of New York, McKinley had chosen Governor Theodore Roosevelt as his vice-presidential running mate for the upcoming1900 election. Again, McKinley ran against William Jennings Bryan. Bryan's position focused on McKinley's views of American imperialism (in regard to the United States' newly acquired territories near Asia,) silver, and the growth of big business and trusts.

McKinley rarely traveled during the election campaigns, as it was considered inappropriate for a president at that time. McKinley sent Roosevelt all over the country making campaign speeches for the Republican ticket and meeting the public. McKinley easily won the election again in 1900.

By 1901, McKinley was concerned about corporate trusts because of their stranglehold on competition and the increased cost of goods to consumers. McKinley actually pursued a policy of reciprocity in which he used tariff negotiations to open up new markets abroad for American goods through bi-lateral tariff reductions.

President McKinley at the 1901 Pan-American Exposition
24-hours before shot

Roosevelt disliked his role as vice president as he felt powerless and merely a puppet of McKinley. However, all this changed when McKinley was shot after delivering a speech at the 1901 Pan-American Exposition in Buffalo, New York on September 6th. McKinley died on September 14 and Roosevelt was sworn in as president the next day.

The photographs and narratives that follow capture a "slice of life" of Governor Theodore Roosevelt on the presidential election campaign trail of 1900, while McKinley stayed at "home" delivering his "front porch" speeches in Washington D.C. and Canton, Ohio.

The Photographs

September 7, 1900

It looks to be a beautiful late summer day in Saginaw, Michigan when Theodore Roosevelt's carriage passed by this crowd. We can see the blatant stares of the people as this photograph was taken. Some of them have very comedic and quizzical looks on their faces.

September 7, 1900

"More fellow Americans"

The number of people in Saginaw, Michigan who came to see and hear Roosevelt speak was impressive. In this photograph, the whole area is packed with wall-to-wall people. Note the mother and child peering out the window in their dwelling above the pharmacy in the rear left-hand corner of the photograph.

September 7, 1900

The presidential entourage made a stop in Kalamazoo, Michigan. Here we see horse-drawn carriages behind the Kalamazoo station. Of particular interest located behind the carriages is a large advertisement for "Buffalo Bill's Wild West Show" with a graphic of men on horseback.

The city of Kalamazoo was a gift to the United States by the Potawatomi Indians in 1827 and permanent settlers came to the land 1829, led by Titus Bronson. When the town was formed, it was originally named "Bronson" after the city's founder. However, he was soon tried and convicted of stealing a cherry tree and villagers demanded the name of the town be changed. By the time Michigan was admitted to the Union in 1837, Bronson was renamed Kalamazoo. The name Kalamazoo is derived from a Potawatomi Indian expression, "Kikalamazoo," meaning "the rapids at the river crossing," or "boiling water."

September 7-9, 1900

"Just a crowd"

This photograph and the one that follows are similar views of a Michigan crowd, although this is from a closer vantage point, showing the crowd cluster and political signs. Three poster signs can clearly be seen, but it is difficult to make out the entire text. The largest poster on the left says "The Sweepstakes of Our Nation" with caricatures of Roosevelt on the left and McKinley on the right. The poster on the right shows an illustration of Roosevelt and reads "We're Right."

September 7-9, 1900

These photographs have captured what today have become part of a lost American culture.

September 7-9, 1900

"The Colonel shaking hands with mounted campaign Rough Riders"

Theodore Roosevelt was quite a showman. He enjoyed publicity and knew how to work a crowd. He was a great public relations person, and this talent was a crucial factor in his 1904 re-election as president.

Roosevelt is seen shaking hands with mounted "campaign" Rough Riders in either Michigan or Indiana in the center of the photograph, with his back turned toward the camera. Along the way, Roosevelt would sometimes exit his carriage to greet the crowds.

September 7-9, 1900

The location where this particular image was taken is unknown, but in all likelihood, it is somewhere in Michigan or Indiana.

The one thing most fascinating about the series of photographs in this volume is the "slice of life" vantage point, which is a lost attribute. These photographs not only display Roosevelt and other adversaries, but also seemingly unimportant happenings, which today have become part of lost American history. For example, we can see what the "wild west" was like at the turn of the 20th century. Drug stores seemed to be a fixture in these few and far between towns (note J.J. Freeman's Drug Store behind the crowd.)

September 11, 1900

"Fellow citizens at Egan"

Here we can see the town name Egan on a sign attached to the building above the large crowd gathered to hear Roosevelt speak. Egan, South Dakota appears to be a small town as there is a lot of open space and sparse structures in the distance on the right-hand side of the photograph.

September 11, 1900

"Campaign Rough Riders – Anywhere"

Theodore Roosevelt had fought in the Spanish-American War in 1898 and held the rank of Colonel. He is most famous for leading his cavalry, known as the "Rough Riders" to victory during the Battle of Kettle Hill. Soon after he returned home, he was elected governor of New York and served until William McKinley won the presidential election of 1900. Roosevelt had now become vice president of the United States.

This photo shows Spanish-American War veterans dressed up in their cavalry uniforms somewhere in South Dakota. Roosevelt was very popular as can be seen by the large turnout of campaign Rough Riders alongside his train.

September 11, 1900

"Elk Point"

Roosevelt made a stop at the Elk Point train depot in South Dakota to greet the waiting people. It is interesting to note the stagecoach at the right rear of the photograph. A good number of people climbed atop the stagecoach to use it as a viewing platform. At first glance, the stagecoach is barely recognizable.

Elk Point, South Dakota was the approximate location where the Lewis & Clark Expedition made camp on August 22, 1804. Elk Point was first settled in 1859 along the military road running from Sioux City to Fort Randall, making it one of the oldest communities in South Dakota.

September 12, 1900

**"Indian band and uniformed school boys from the reservation
near Chamberlain, S. Dakota"**

A band comprised of Native Americans dressed in uniform from
a Chamberlain, South Dakota reservation in preparation for Roosevelt's
arrival. They stand proud with the American flag displayed in the foreground. Many of the smaller children hold American flags in their hands
as well.

September 12, 1900

As the carriage arrived closer to its final destination, the crowds would make way for it to pass. Before President McKinley was assassinated, it was easy for crowds to come within inches of a presidential candidate. McKinley was assassinated in 1901 while making a speech at the Pan American Exhibition in Buffalo, NY shortly after this western campaign tour. Eleven years later on October 14, 1912, while Roosevelt was campaigning for president in Milwaukee, Wisconsin, an angry saloonkeeper named John F. Schrank shot him in the chest. Amazingly, Roosevelt's steel eyeglass case and the thickness of his speech manuscript contained in his coat pocket slowed the bullet enough to prevent this wound from becoming fatal. He continued his speech for another hour and a half before seeking medical attention.

Men and women of all ages came to see Roosevelt as he made his way to his destination. In this photograph he is arriving in Chamberlain, South Dakota. It is obvious from the photograph he is well received. A uniformed band is standing ready to greet him at the left of the photo.

September 12, 1900

     This photograph is another view of the previous photograph with a slightly different vantage point. The American flag is flying, and the bunting decoration also shows a pattern of the stars and stripes in the right foreground. There is a coal/lumber yard owned by a James A. Smith behind the gathering crowd.

September 12, 1900

"Squaw & papoose, American mother and child"

This photograph is notably interesting because it contrasts a Native American mother and her child with an American mother and child. The inscription on the back of the original photo clearly points this out. Note the crutches the Native American mother is holding, along with the many layers of clothing she is wearing, all while she carries her "papoose."

September 12, 1900

"Indians at Chamberlain much interested"

Native Americans gathering in fair numbers are eager to hear Roosevelt speak in Chamberlain, South Dakota. Again, we see them in western dress. To the right of the crowd, you will see Dr. R. C. Drake's dental office and Scott's Drug Store.

September 12, 1900

**"Real Rough Riders – Cow Boys Charging after the Train at
Chamberlain South Dakota"**

Theodore Roosevelt was one of America's most popular presidents. You can see the excitement stirred by the news of Roosevelt's campaign tour leaving Chamberlain, South Dakota by the sheer number of cowboys on horses that have come to follow his presidential train. Roosevelt made many stops on his way out west, but the Dakotas were his favorite. He had lived in North Dakota for some years at his Medora ranch before returning to New York in 1884. Oyster Bay, Long Island, would become his permanent home, except while he resided in the White House from 1901-1909.

This photo was taken from the back of the presidential train. It is highlighting the delight on the cowboys' faces as the train passed through the town, making its way from the station.

September 13, 1900

"The Colonel speaking at Woonsocket"

Pictured is a wonderful photograph depicting Theodore Roosevelt on stage just after speaking to a full crowd in the town of Woonsocket, South Dakota.

The name Woonsocket is Native American for "thunder mist." Native American tribes including the Nipmucs, Wampanoag, and Narragansett originally inhabited Woonsocket. European settlers first arrived in Woonsocket in the 17th century and harnessed the power of the Woonsocket Falls for agriculture. In the 18th century, Woonsocket, Rhode Island became an industrial powerhouse because of its vast water supply.

By the mid-1800s, Woonsocket was famous as one of this country's largest textile manufacturers.

The city of Woonsocket, South Dakota was formed in 1883 at the junction of the Chicago, Milwaukee, and Saint Paul Railroads. It got its name from C.H. Prior, superintendent of the railroad, who named the new town Woonsocket, after his hometown of Woonsocket, Rhode Island.

September 13, 1900

"Col. Lee Stover of So. Dakota"

Lee Stover of South Dakota served as a volunteer Lieutenant Colonel in the US Army 1st Infantry Division from April 25, 1898 - October 5, 1899, during the Spanish-American War and shortly thereafter. This photograph captures Colonel Stover in his war uniform as he gives a speech to the crowd below. This photograph and the three others that follow were taken in Watertown, South Dakota.

What a sight it must have been to see such important people speaking amidst the euphoria the country was experiencing after winning the war against Spain. The crowd is enormous, and the available rooftops are completely filled with spectators anxious to view the day's activities.

September 13, 1900

"The Colonel speaking"

This photograph really captures the essence of Roosevelt's speech mannerisms. He was quite animated and emphasized his points with hand gestures.

The J.I. Case Threshing Machine Company and the Mitchell Wagons Company provide the backdrop for Roosevelt's speech. Jerome Increase Case in Rochester, Wisconsin established the J.I. CASE COMPANY in 1842. By 1844 he built a factory in Racine, Wisconsin. In 1886, the J.I. Case Company was the world's largest manufacturer of steam engines and by the turn of the century was selling farm tractors. By 1904, Case was producing more steam engines and threshing machines than its competition. Case is still operating today under the same name but has been purchased and sold off by other companies over the last century.

Mitchell Wagons (originally known as Mitchell and Lewis Wagon Company) was founded in 1834 by Henry Mitchell and William T. Lewis of Racine, Wisconsin. They were well known for building farm wagons by the turn of the century and were generally sold through John Deere dealerships at that time. John Deere eventually purchased the company in 1911.

September 13, 1900

"Senator Knute Nelson of Minnesota"

Here is the same view of the stage, this time with Senator Knute Nelson of Minnesota speaking. Knute Nelson was involved in politics for most of his life. He became governor of Minnesota in 1892 and was re-elected in 1894. He resigned as governor when he became elected as a senator on January 31, 1895. He was re-elected as Senator in 1900, 1906, 1912, and 1918. He served as U.S. senator until his death on April 28th, 1923.

September 13, 1900

"Gov Shaw of Iowa Speaking"

Next up to the podium is Governor Leslie Mortimer Shaw of Iowa, who served from 1898-1902. Shortly after he retired as governor of Iowa, Roosevelt appointed Shaw as Secretary of the Treasury (1902-1907,) mainly because he was a strong Roosevelt supporter and defended the gold standard during the presidential campaign of 1896. Governor Shaw also believed the Treasury should contribute during hard times via the use of Treasury funds. He bought back government bonds from the commercial banks that owned them and increased the number of government depository banks. In 1902 banks were no longer required to maintain cash reserves against their holdings of public funds. The goal was to provide a more elastic currency when the market was weak. In 1907, Shaw resigned from his post as governor to become a banker in New York.

September 13, 1900

Rough Riders/Campaign at Watertown"

In this photo, Roosevelt's train is departing the Watertown, South Dakota train station. It is amazing to see the plethora of people following the presidential train as it makes its way from town to town. Notice again the campaign Rough Riders, some of whom are carrying flags for this special presidential event. This photograph really captures a bygone era.

September 16, 1900

"Real Americans with pipe of peace"

Native Americans were quite interested in Roosevelt's speeches when he came through their part of the country in the Dakotas. However, Roosevelt did not believe Native Americans, African Americans, and Asians were equal to white people. He felt people of "color" were a burden that the "white man" must carry as part of his Christian duty. His "Square Deal" called for political reform in the United Sates, but critics have said this was offset by his racist views.

This photograph, taken in Hebron, North Dakota, is quite significant as it captures Native Americans holding a peace pipe. Note how they are dressed in western attire. We can only guess at what they are pondering.

September 16, 1900

**"Old friends meeting the Colonel at his old ranch station, Medora
in the Bad Lands on the Little Missouri River, No. Dakota"**

Theodore Roosevelt bought a ranch in North Dakota in 1883. After the death of his first wife Alice Lee and his mother in 1884, he spent many years at the ranch engaging in buffalo hunts and enjoying the scenic beauty of the Bad Lands. Roosevelt once said, "I never would have been president if it had not been for my experiences in North Dakota." It was the natural beauty of the Bad Lands that inspired Roosevelt to dedicate much of his life to fighting for conservation of America's wilderness. He was responsible for initiating the Antiquities Act that created Devil's Tower of Wyoming, the first national monument in 1906.

A crowd of people is awaiting the arrival of the Colonel at Roosevelt's Medora, North Dakota ranch train station, which is located in the Bad Lands. Visible are the rock formations at the right-hand corner of the photograph.

September 16, 1900

Roosevelt's train made many stops while enroute. Many times, he would speak directly from the back of the caboose when there was no formal stage. These speeches became known as "whistle stops." Although this photograph is out of focus, we can make out Roosevelt on the right with his hands in his pockets. The other man is Joseph A Ferris. Ferris was the owner of the Ferris Milk & Cream Co., a wholesale company he started in 1866 at 293 Greenwich St, New York.

Perhaps Roosevelt is just getting ready to make a speech to the spectators below. The town in which this speech was made is Medora, North Dakota.

September 17, 1900

"Curtis Guild Jr."

This photograph shows a curious looking Curtis Guild Jr., Roosevelt's right-hand man during his 1900 campaign tour, in Montana. Guild actually spoke for Roosevelt when Roosevelt lost his voice. Both the photographer of this picture and the circumstances of the moment captured are unknown. Guild may have been simply laughing or looking at something comical. In his right hand, he is holding a small floral arrangement, perhaps a boutonniere.

Curtis Guild Jr. was a lieutenant colonel in the Spanish-American War of 1898. He became the Republican lieutenant governor of Massachusetts from 1903-1905, and then Republican governor from 1906-1909. He was appointed special United States ambassador to Russia from 1911-1913.

September 17, 1900

"Western way of hitching a horse"

The horse is standing all by itself, unattached and the humorous inscription on the back says, "western way of hitching a horse." In the background of the photograph are various buildings of retail trade. This photograph was taken in Billings, Montana where there are both furniture and tool merchants with many horse-drawn wagons out front and a saloon next to the tool store.

September 17, 1900

"A western Waldorf Astoria"

The Hotel McIntyre, in Montana, is clearly the focal point in this photograph. There is little to no real estate development beside the hotel, but we can see scantily laid out buildings and windmills in the distance. The horses hitched to the posts in front of the hotel suggest that a few guests are staying there. Was it possible that Roosevelt stayed here? Or was this photograph the butt of one of the photographer's jokes when it was inscribed "a western Waldorf Astoria" on the back?

September 17, 1900

**"A dressed up Sunday afternoon Montana group –
just to see us go by."**

A packed, yet curious group of Columbus, Montana onlookers
form behind the presidential train to catch a glimpse as it passes by on a
sunny afternoon. Something of this caliber would most certainly bring
the town folks out to get a first-hand view of this country's next president.
These events drew hoards of spectators since the only news about the
presidential candidates in 1900 was in print.

September 17, 1900

"Bozeman, the highest station."

Another stop along Roosevelt's campaign trail was Bozeman, Montana. The town of Bozeman was commissioned on July 7, 1864, by Daniel E. Rouse and William J. Beall and formally named on August 9, 1864. The town was named after John Bozeman who led settlers across a roadway called the Bozeman Trail, which was the northern spur of the Oregon Trail. Bozeman was a wagonmaster and trail guide who envisioned the town as a prime area for farming and a central supply stop for miners of the Gold Rush. The Bozeman Trail began at Landrock and ended at Virginia City, Montana. It was open for three years until the Sioux and Cheyenne Indian tribes shut it down to halt the immigration of new settlers into the area.

September 18, 1900

"Real cowboys saluting"

As Roosevelt's entourage came through the various stop points, he was greeted by all kinds of people. In this case, we see "real" cowboys taking their hats off to salute him as he passed through Idaho. Also, note the group of men standing atop the railroad cars (that say Chicago, Milwaukee, St. Paul) for a better view.

September 18, 1900

"A So Dakota crowd"

While this photograph caption and the one that follows mentions the location as So Dakota, research shows these scenes to actually be in Idaho. Women were given the right to vote in state elections in Idaho and Utah as early as 1896. You will note in the following photograph there are "Lady Rough Riders" in what appears to be Spanish-American War uniforms.

The street is mobbed with curious onlookers and decorated for Roosevelt's arrival with bunting and American flags. One of the signs in the crowd reads "Let Well Enough Alone," most likely referring to the incumbent President McKinley. Behind the crowd is a clothing merchant and the Rich Brothers establishment.

Roosevelt's popularity is quite evident and continued for many years later, despite his losing the 1912 presidential election to Woodrow Wilson.

September 18, 1900

"So Dakota "Lady" Rough Riders in back of a crowd"

  Here is another view of the previous photograph, albeit with more contrast and from a different angle. The Rich Brothers building with the American flag is visible again on the right with a photography studio next door on the left, but now we can see what looms across the street along with the full depth of the crowd. If we look carefully toward the back of the photograph, mounted "Lady Rough Riders" can be seen trotting behind the crowd in full support of Governor Roosevelt.

September 18, 1900

"Fellow Americans"

This photograph depicts the sheer size of the crowds that formed to greet Theodore Roosevelt in Idaho. Roosevelt's campaign tour of 1900 was just 2 years after the United States' victory in our war against Spain. He is considered a hero and well remembered to this day for leading his cavalry of "Rough Riders" up Kettle Hill during the battle of Santiago, thus ending the war in July 1898.

Although difficult to see with the naked eye, there is a building in the background with an American flag and a sign which in part reads "Teddy went to Cuba, Billy (McKinley) stayed at home, Teddy will get the roasted pig, Billy can pick the bone," thus making reference to Roosevelt's hero status in America's war with Spain.

September 18, 1900

"The Colonel Smiles"

Theodore Roosevelt was a great speaker. He loved crowds and took advantage of those opportunities. He spoke with much animation and vigor, using many hand gestures, especially clenching his fists to make a point.

Although Roosevelt was not the first presidential candidate to have his speeches recorded, his speeches are most memorable. The first president to be commercially recorded was William Howard Taft. Roosevelt made recordings for Edison and the Victor Talking Machine Company regarding important issues of the day. For a man of his great stature, it is ironic that his voice was soft, yet eloquent.

In this close up photograph, Roosevelt is smiling for the crowd. People have filled in all available space and gathered on building rooftops and telephone poles. This photograph was most likely taken in Idaho.

September 18, 1900

"Lady" Rough Riders close-up as escort taken from our carriage"

While campaigning, Roosevelt would ride in a horse-drawn open carriage to feel more up close and personal as well as tip his hat to the crowd. This photograph taken from the presidential carriage in Idaho is interesting because we see women dressed in "rough rider" style hats on horseback as a tribute to Roosevelt's heroism in the Spanish-American War. Also, take note of the male war veteran behind the lady on the extreme right of the photograph, fully dressed in uniform. The American flag stands proudly in the foreground.

September 19, 1900

"The Colonel shaking hands with Spanish war veterans, No. Dakota"

Although impossible to see, we know this photograph is of Roosevelt shaking hands with Spanish War veterans somewhere in North Dakota, from the inscription written on the back of the image. The war veterans wearing their cavalry hats flank Roosevelt. It must have been a special moment for these veterans to shake the hand of Roosevelt the war hero. Even two years after the war was over, Roosevelt was still referred to as the "Colonel."

Again, we have another labeling error on the photograph. Research suggests this location is most likely Portacello, Idaho.

September 22-24, 1900

"To towers and chimney tops"

The roof is literally covered with diehard Wyoming spectators, as there is no more room to stand comfortably to see Theodore Roosevelt speak. Standing or sitting wherever one could find a spot was a common practice in those days, but with new laws and restrictions, this practice became illegal in many cities because of the inherent dangers.

September 26, 1900

"Leadville, Colorado – The saddle was just presented to the Colonel"

Roosevelt traveled the western states during the campaign of 1900 and sometimes received gifts from the various town officials. Here the crowd has gathered outside a courthouse in Leadville, Colorado, where Roosevelt was presented with a saddle, which sits on the stage railing to the right.

Bibliography

Bozeman Chamber of Commerce, "History and Trivia About the Bozeman Area," http://www.bozemancvb.visitmt.com/history-trivia.html

Case Corporation, "Company History- The Early Years," 2002, http://www.casecorp.com/corporate/history/index.html

Cortez, Jan, "Jan's Digs," State and County Information Links, http://www.jansdigs.com/Racine/belleflmitchell.html

Devils Tower National Monument, Discovery Computing, Inc, 2001, http://www.newyoming.com/DevilsTower/

Discover ND, Your Gateway to North Dakota, "THEODORE ROOSEVELT: Bully for North Dakota!," 1998 http://www.ndtourism.com/regions/west/WestRoosevelt.html

Elk Point, http://www.elkpoint.org/

Harvard University Library, "Impressions of the Campaign - Detroit, Michigan to Pueblo Colorado: Guide," 2007 http://oasis.lib.harvard.edu/oasis/deliver/~trc00034

KalamazooMI.com "There's something for you in Kalamazoo!," http://www.kalamazoomi.com/hisf.htm

Kestenbaum, Lawrence. "The Political Graveyard, A Historical Database of Political Cemeteries," July 14, 2002, http://political-graveyard.com/index.html

Linke, Paula. "City of Woonsocket – The Town with the Beautiful Lake," August 26, 2008,
http://www.woonsocketsd.com/index.html

McKinley Memorial Library, "William McKinley – 25th President of the United States," 1999,
http://www.mckinley.lib.oh.us/McKinley/biography.htm

MinnesotaPolitics.net, August 9, 2002, http://minnesotapolitics.net/Governors/12Nelson.htm

Thayer, William Roscoe, "Theodore Roosevelt, an intimate biography," Boston: Houghton Mifflin, 1919.

Theodore Roosevelt Association, "Keeping the Spirit Alive," July 27, 2002, http://www.theodoreroosevelt.org/

Kunhardt, Philip B.., Philip B. Kunhardt III, and Peter W. Kunhardt, "The American President," April 2000, http://www.americanpresident.org/kotrain/courses/TR/TR_In_Brief.htm

Rhode Island Economic Development Corporation, "City of Woonsocket," http://www.riedc.com/mcds/Woonsocket.html

Robinson, Doane. "History of South Dakota Volume 1," 1904, http://searches1.rootsweb.com/usgenweb/archives/sd/military/spam/lxxvi.txt

Thompson, Katie L., "The Wagon Wheels Go 'Round," Field Reporter.com, January 29, 2001, http://www.field-reporter.com/The_Green_Girl_2001/gg-01-29-01.htm

United States Department of the Treasury, "Secretaries of the Treasury – Leslie M. Shaw," 2001, http://www.treas.gov/curator/secretary/shaw.htm

Woonsocket, My Home Town on the Web, "Growth of an Industrial City,"

<u>Appendix A</u>

Unidentified Photographs in the Collection

Presidential campaigning by railroad became quite popular at the turn of the 20th century. Theodore Roosevelt was the first president to use the railroad as a platform for making speeches while on presidential tours. This practice continued into the mid-20th century, with the most famous practitioner being Roosevelt's cousin, Franklin.

Theodore Roosevelt was a president of many firsts, including being the first to ride in and own a car, fly in an airplane, be submerged in a submarine, to win the Nobel Peace Prize, and to travel outside of the U.S. borders while in office. He went to Panama during the building of the Panama Canal.

When crowds were gathering in the various towns, Roosevelt often disembarked from his train to a presidential carriage where he would frequently stand and tip his hat to the crowds that followed alongside the carriage. Usually, the carriage had a destination to where the presidential candidate would make formal speeches in front of large crowds. The building to the extreme right of the photograph is a wholesale liquor store.

The location where this photograph was taken is unknown.

Here is another view of Roosevelt in his carriage on his way to make a speech. There are several carriages in this photograph, each with a number card hanging from a gas headlamp. Roosevelt's carriage is number 1 and in front of his to the right is carriage number 6.

It was obvious that he was expected to pass through this town because we can see the bunting decoration wrapped around a pole in the foreground. There is a Union Pacific train car centered directly behind the action. To the upper-right we see a building with white lettering that says Lime Cement.

It is a crowded, bright sunny day as Roosevelt speaks to the large crowd below the stage. He is clearly seen to the right-hand side of the stage. The vantage point of this photograph shows the makeshift timber log stage on which Roosevelt speaks to his eager fans. The other men behind him are unknown. The stage is decorated in "stars and stripes"

<u>Appendix B</u>

Transcriptions of the Theodore Roosevelt Speeches

Scott Malawski

National Phonograph Company

Edison 4-Minute Wax Amberols – August 1912

The Progressive Covenant with the People

Political parties exist to secure responsible government and to execute the will of the people. From these great tasks both of the old parties have turned aside. Instead of instruments to promote the general welfare, they have become the tools of corrupt interests, which use them impartially to serve their selfish purposes. Behind the ostensible government sits enthroned an invisible government owing no allegiance and acknowledging no responsibility to the people. To destroy this invisible government, to dissolve the unholy alliance between corrupt businesses and corrupt politics, is the first task of the statesmanship of the day. Unhampered by tradition, uncorrupted by power, undismayed by the magnitude of the task, the new party offers itself as the instrument of the people, to sweep away old abuses, to build a new and nobler government.

This declaration is our covenant with the people and we hereby bind the party and its candidates, in state and nation, to the pledges made herein. With all my heart and soul, with every particle of high purpose that is within me, I pledge you my word to do everything I can to put every particle of courage, of common sense, and of strength that I have at your disposal, and to endeavor so far as strength has given me to live up to the obligations you have put upon me, and to endeavor to carry out in the interest of our whole people the policies to which you have today solemnly dedicated yourselves in the name of the millions of men and women for whom you speak.

Surely there never was a fight better worth making than the one in which we are engaged. It little matters what befalls any one of us who for the time being stand in the forefront of the battle. I hope we shall win, and I believe that if we can wake the people to what the fight really means, we shall win. But win or lose, we shall not falter. Whatever fate may at the moment overtake any of us, the movement itself will not stop. Our cause is based on the eternal principles of righteousness; even though we who now lead may for the time fail, in the end the cause itself shall triumph. Six weeks ago, here in Chicago, I spoke to the honest representatives of a convention which was not dominated by honest men. A convention wherein sat, alas, a majority of men who, with sneering indifference to every principle of right, so acted as to bring to a shameful end a party which had been founded over half a century ago by men in whose souls burned the fire of lofty endeavor. Now to you men, who, in your turn, have come together to spend and be spent in the endless crusade against wrong, to you who face the future resolute and confident, to you who strive in a spirit of brotherhood for the betterment of our nation, to you who gird yourselves for this great new fight in the never-ending warfare for the good of human- kind, I say in closing what in that speech I said in closing: we stand at Armageddon, and we battle for the Lord.

Social and Industrial Justice

Our prime concern is that in dealing with the fundamental law of the land, and assuming finally to interpret it and therefore finally to make it, the acts of the courts should be subject to and not above the final control of the people as a whole. I deny that the American people have surrendered to any set of men, no matter what their position or their character, the final right to determine those fundamental questions upon which free self-government ultimately depends. The people themselves must be the ultimate makers of their own constitution, and where their agents differ in their interpretations of the constitution, the people themselves should be given the chance, after full and deliberate judgment, authoritatively to settle what interpretation it is that their representatives shall thereafter adopt as binding. We do not question the general honesty of the courts, but in applying to present-day social conditions the general prohibitions that were intended originally as safeguards to the citizen against the arbitrary power of government in the hands of caste and privilege, these prohibitions have been turned by the courts from safeguards against political and social privilege into barriers against political and social justice and advancement. Our purpose is not to impugn the courts, but to emancipate them from a position where they stand in the way of social justice, and to emancipate the people in an orderly way from the inequity of enforced submission to a doctrine which would turn constitutional provisions, which were intended to favor social justice and advancement, into prohibitions against such justice and advancement.

In the last twenty years an increasing percentage of our people have come to depend on industry for their livelihood, so that today the wage-workers in industry rank in importance side by side to the tillers of the soil. As a people, we cannot afford to let any group of citizens or any individual citizen, live or labor under conditions which are injurious to the common welfare. Industry, therefore, must submit to such public regulation as will make it a means of life and health, not of death or inefficiency. We must protect the crushable elements at the base of our present industrial structure. We stand for a living wage. Wages are subnormal if they fail to provide a living for those who devote their time and energy to industrial occupations. The monetary equivalent of a living wage varies according to local conditions, but must include enough to secure the elements of a normal standard of living—a standard high enough to make morality possible, to provide for education and recreation, to care for immature members of the family, to maintain the family during periods of sickness, and to permit a reasonable savings for old age. Hours are excessive if they fail to afford the worker sufficient time to recuperate and return to his work thoroughly refreshed. We hold that the night labor of women and children is abnormal and should be prohibited; we hold that the employment of women over forty-eight hours per week is abnormal and should be prohibited. We hold the seven-day working week is abnormal, and we hold that one day of rest in seven should be provided by law. We hold that the continuous industries, operating twenty-four hours out of twenty-four, are abnormal, and where, because of public necessity or for technical reasons such as molten metal, the twenty-four hours must be divided into two shifts of twelve hours or three shifts of eight, they should by law be divided into three of eight.

The Farmer and the Business Man

There is no body of our people whose interests are more inextricably interwoven with the interests of all the people than is the case with the farmers. The Country Life Commission should be revived with greatly increased powers; its abandonment was a severe blow to the interests of our people. The welfare of the farmer is a basic need of this nation. It is the men from the farm who in the past have taken the lead in every great movement within this nation, whether in time of war or in time of peace. It is well to have our cities prosper, but it is not well if they prosper at the expense of the country. In this movement the lead must be taken by the farmers themselves; but our people as a whole, through their governmental agencies, should back the farmers. Everything possible should be done to better the economic condition of the farmer, and also to increase the social value of the life of the farmer, the farmer's wife, and their children. The burdens of labor and loneliness bear heavily on the women in the country; their welfare should be the especial concern of all of us. Everything possible should be done to make life in the country profitable so as to be attractive from the economic standpoint and there should be just the same chance to live as full, as well rounded, and as highly useful lives in the country as in the city.

The government must cooperate with the farmer to make the farm more productive. There must be no skinning of the soil. The farm should be left for the farmer's son in better and not worse condition because of its cultivation. Moreover, every invention and improvement, every discovery and economy, should be at the service of the farmer in the work of production. And in addition, he should be helped to cooperate in business fashion with these fellows, so that the money paid by the consumer for the product of the soil shall, to as large a degree as possible, go into the pockets of the man who raised that product from the soil. So long as the farmer leaves cooperative activities with their profit-sharing to the city man of business, so long will the foundations of wealth be undermined and the comforts of enlightenment be impossible in the country communities.

The present conditions of business cannot be accepted as satisfactory. There are too many who do not prosper enough, and of the few who prosper greatly there are certainly some whose prosperity does not mean well for the country. Rational Progressives, no matter how radical, are well aware that nothing the government can do will make some men prosper. And we heartily approve the prosperity, no matter how great, of any man, if it comes as an incident to rendering service to the community; but we wish to shape conditions so that a greater number of the small men in business—the decent, respectable, industrious, and energetic men who conduct small businesses, who are retail traders, who run small stores and shops—shall be able to succeed, and so that the big man who is dishonest, shall not be allowed to succeed at all.

Our aim is to control business, not to strangle it—and above all, not to continue a policy of make-believe strangle towards big concerns that do evil, and constant menace toward both big and little concerns that do well. Our aim is to promote prosperity and then to see that prosperity is passed around, that there is a proper division of prosperity. We wish to control big business so as to secure among other things good wages for the wageworkers and reasonable prices for the consumers. We will not submit to the prosperity that is obtained by lowering the wages of working men and charging an excessive price to consumers, nor to that other kind of prosperity obtained by swindling investors or getting unfair advantages over business rivals. We propose to make it worth while for our business men to develop the most efficient business agencies, but we propose to make these business agencies do complete justice to our whole people. We're against crooked business, big or little. We are in favor of honest business, big or little. We propose to penalize conduct and not size.

The Right of the People to Rule

The great fundamental issue now before our people can be stated briefly. It is, "Are the American people fit to govern themselves, to rule themselves, to control themselves?" I believe they are; my opponents do not. I believe in the right of the people to rule. I believe that the majority of the plain people of the United States will, day in and day out, make fewer mistakes in governing themselves than any smaller class or body of men, no matter what their training, will make in trying to govern them. I believe, again, that the American people are, as a whole, capable of self-control, and of learning by their mistakes.

Our opponents pay lip-loyalty to this doctrine, but they show their real beliefs by the way in which they champion every device to make the nominal rule of the people a sham. I am not leading this fight as a matter of aesthetic pleasure. I am leading because somebody must lead or else the fight would not be made at all. I prefer to work with moderate, with rational-conservatives, provided only that they do in good faith strive forward towards the light. But when they halt and turn their backs to the light and sit with the scorners on the seats of reaction, then I must part company with them. We the people cannot turn back. Our aim must be steady, wise progress.

It would be well if all people would study the history of a sister republic. All the woes of France for a century and a quarter have been due to the folly of her people in splitting into two camps of unreasonable conservatism and unreasonable radicalism. Had pre- revolutionary France listened to men like Turgot and backed them up, all would have gone well. But the beneficiaries of privilege, the Bourbon reactionaries, the shortsighted ultra-conservatives, turned down Turgot and then found that instead of him they had obtained Robespierre. They gained twenty years freedom from all restraint and reform, at the cost of the whirlwind of the "red terror" and in their turn the unbridled extremists of the terror induced a blind reaction. And so, with convulsion and oscillation from one extreme to another, with alternations of violent radicalism and violent Bourbonism, the French people went through misery toward a shattered goal. May we profit from the experiences of our fellow republicans across the water, and go forward steadily, avoiding all wild extremes; and may our ultra-conservatives remember that the rule of the Bourbons brought on the revolution, and may our would-be revolutionaries remember that no Bourbon was ever such a dangerous enemy of the people and their freedom as the professed friend of both, Robespierre.

There is no danger of a revolution in this country; but there is grave discontent and unrest, and in order to remove them there is need of all the wisdom and probity and deep- seated faith in and purpose to uplift humanity we have at our command. Friends, our task as Americans is to strive for social and industrial justice, achieved through the genuine rule of the people. This is our end, our purpose. The methods for achieving the end are merely expedients, to be finally accepted or rejected, according as actual experience shows that they work well or ill. But in our hearts we must have this lofty purpose, and strive for it in all earnestness and sincerity, or our work will come to nothing. In order to succeed we need leaders of inspired idealism, leaders to whom are granted great visions, who dream greatly and strive to make their dreams come true; who can kindle the people with the fire from their own burning souls. The leader for the time being, whoever he may be, is but an instrument, to be used until broken and then to be cast aside; and if he is worth his salt he will care no more when he is broken than a soldier cares where he is sent, where his life is proffered in order that the victory may be won. In the long fight for righteousness the watchword for all of us is "spend and be spent."

Victor Talking Machine Company - September 1912

The Liberty of the People

The difference between Mr. Wilson and myself is fundamental. The other day in a speech at Sioux Falls, Mr. Wilson stated his position when he said that the history of government, the history of liberty, was the history of the limitation of governmental power. This is true as an academic statement of history in the past. It is not true as a statement affecting the present. It is true of the history of medieval Europe. It is not true of the history of 20th century America. In the days when all governmental power existed exclusively in the King or in the baronage, and when the people had no shred of that power in their own hand, then it undoubtedly was true that the history of liberty was the history of the limitation of the governmental power of the outsiders who possessed that power. But today, the people have actually or potentially the entire governmental power. It is theirs to use and to exercise if they choose to use and to exercise it. It offers the only adequate instrument with which they can work for the betterment, for the uplifting, of the masses of our people. The liberty of which Mr. Wilson speaks today means merely the liberty of some great trust magnate to do that which he is not entitled to do. It means merely the liberty of some factory owner to work haggard women over hours for under pay and himself to pocket the proceeds. It means the liberty of the factory owner who crowds his operatives into some crazy deathtrap on a top floor, where if fire starts the slaughter is immense. It means the liberty of the big factory owner who is conscienceless and unscrupulous, to work his men and women under conditions which eat into their lives like an acid. It means the liberty of even less conscientious factory owners to make their money out of the toil, the labor, of little children. Men of this stamp are the men whose liberty would be preserved by Mr. Wilson. Men of this stamp are the men whose liberty would be preserved by the limitation of governmental power. We propose, on the contrary, to extend governmental power in order to secure the liberty of the wage- workers, of the men and women who toil in industry, to save the liberty of the oppressed from the oppressor. Mr. Wilson stands for the liberty of the oppressor to oppress; we stand for the limitation of his liberty thus to oppress those who are weaker than himself.

Mr. Roosevelt Pays His Respects to Penrose and Archbold

In this contest, we have a right to appeal to all honest men to support us without regard to what their political affiliations may have been in the past. The powers that prey are united against us. The powers that prey pay no heed to a question of partisanships in this contest. Some of them may, individually, prefer Mr. Wilson to Mr. Taft and others may prefer Mr. Taft to Mr. Wilson. But the preference for either is tepid compared to the intensity of their animosity towards us, and their willingness to stand by either of the other two candidates or by anyone else, if only they can beat the Progressive party. The reason is evident, these men, the big bosses of the political field, the beneficiaries of privilege in the field of industry, the men who represent that sinister alliance between crooked politics and crooked business, which has done more than anything else for the corruption of American life, are united as one man against the genuine rule of the people themselves.

The privileged classes, the representatives of special privilege, of special interests, can always make terms with a boss or bosses. They can make terms with the bosses who dominate the Republican party, they can make terms with the bosses who dominate the Democratic party, but they can't make terms with the people. They can't make terms with the men who honestly and genuinely represent the popular will. The attitude of our opponents has been well shown by the alliance between Messrs. Penrose and Archbold. You may remember that the other day, Senator Penrose of Pennsylvania and Mr. Archbold of the Standard Oil Company appeared before a senate committee to testify against me. That is, nominally, they were to testify against me. Really, they were testifying against Mr. Cornelius Bliss who is dead. Mr. Bliss was the Treasurer of the Republican National Committee during the lifetime of President McKinley and he continued in that position until after 1904 when I ran for President. He lived for seven years after the events as to which these two men have testified. While he lived they never dared open their mouths against him, but now he is dead and the two valiant souls come forward to bear witness against a dead man.

The "Abyssinian Treatment" of Standard Oil

What was really interesting in their testimony, however, was the sidelight it cast on their own motives and standard of propriety, and incidentally, an unwitting tribute to the attitude of my administration. If you will turn to Page 133 of the Record. You can get the record, I will say incidentally, from your senator, unless he's a stands-pat senator in which place, you probably can't get it from him. If you will turn to Page 133 of the Record, you will find where Mr. Archbold says, substantially, "Darkest Abyssinia can show nothing to compare with the treatment administered to the Standard Oil Corporation during the administration of President Roosevelt."

In this instance, Mr. Archbold is testifying to what is quite correct. I did administer the Abyssinian treatment to the Standard Oil Corporation while I was president. I administered it because I thought The Standard Oil needed it. And if ever I am president again, and the Standard Oil or any other corporation acts as the Standard Oil then did, I'll administer the Abyssinian treatment to it again. That's why Mr. Archbold and Mr. Penrose are trying to beat me and to beat the Progressive party. You may notice that Mr. Archbold doesn't complain that the present administration ever administered the Abyssinian treatment to the Standard Oil Company. Not a bit of it. Mr. Archbold has no fear that either the Democratic or Republican parties, if successful at the next election, would administer the Abyssinian treatment to the Standard Oil Corporation or to any other of the big law breaking trusts.

Mr. Archbold knows that the Standard Oil could make its peace with, could come to an agreement with, the men who manage the Republican party or the men who manage the Democratic party, but he also knows that he could make no peace with the leaders of the Progressive party, and he could make no peace with the Progressive party itself because it is in very fact the party of the people of the United States. Again, on the next page of the testimony, you will find where Mr. Bliss is quoted by Mr. Archbold as saying that he had no influence with me. That he could not stop my proceedings at the time when, as Mr. Archbold says, I was engaged in administering the Abyssinian treatment to the Standard Oil Corporation.

Why the Trusts and Bosses Oppose the Progressive Party

Now this statement of Mr. Archbold represents but part of the truth. Mr. Bliss did have real and great influence with me. I respected him and admired him. I should have paid heed to any request or suggestion he made, would have carefully considered it and would have earnestly desired to adopt it, if I honorably could. But it is perfectly true that neither Mr. Bliss nor any other human being ever had any influence over me so far as concerned getting me to abandon the prosecution of any corporation or any individual engaged in wrong doing. To this extent, Mr. Archbold's testimony is entirely true, and I call your attention to the fact that Mr. Archbold and Mr. Penrose come forward to testify against me only because at the moment, I am heading the Progressive movement.

Were I a private citizen, it wouldn't enter their heads to make any assault on me. They dislike me, I grant you, and the longer I live the greater cause I shall give them to dislike me. But that isn't the fundamental motive that's influencing them. The fundamental motive that induces them to act as they have acted in this matter is, not merely that they dislike me, but far more because they dread you. They dread you, the people. You and those like you who make up the people of the United States. They know that their time has come once the people obtain real power.

We stand for the rights of the people. We stand for the rights of the wage-worker. We stand for his right to a living wage. We stand for the right and duty of the government to limit the hours of women in industry, to abolish child labor, to shape the conditions of life and living so that the average wage worker shall be able so to lead his own life and so to support his wife and his children that these children shall grow up into men and women fit for the exacting duties of American citizenship. The

74

big trust magnates of the type of Mr. Archbold, the big politicians of the old boss type so well represented by Mr. Penrose, stand against the people. They object to the government, to government being used primarily in the interest of the people themselves. Naturally, they will do all they can to breakdown the only real enemies that they have and the only real champions, the only real and efficient champions of popular right, and economic, social, and industrial justice.

The Farmer and the Business Man

The welfare of our people is vitally and intimately concerned with the welfare of the farmer. The Country Life Commission should be revived with greatly increased power. Its abandonment was a severe blow to the interest of our nation, for the welfare of the farmer is a basic need of this nation. It is the men from the farms who in the past have taken the lead in every great movement within our country, whether in time of war or in time of peace. It is well to have our cities prosper, but it is not well if they prosper at the expense of the country. In this movement, the lead must be taken by the farmers themselves. But our people as a whole, through their governmental agency should back them up. Everything possible should be done for the better economic condition of the farmer and also to increase the social value of the life of the farmer's wife and their children, no less than of the farmer himself. The burdens of labor and loneliness bear heavily on the women in the country. Their welfare should be the especial concern of all of us. Everything possible should be done to make life in the country profitable so as to be attractive from an economic standpoint, and there should be just the same chance to live as full, as well-rounded, and as useful lives in the country as in the city.

The government must cooperate with the farmer to make the farm more productive. There must be no skinning of the soil. The farm should be left to the farmer's son, in better and not worse condition because of its cultivation. Moreover, every invention and improvement, every discovery and economy, should be at the service of the farmer in the work of production and in addition, he should be helped to cooperate in business fashion with his fellows so that the money paid to the consumer for the product of the soil, shall to as large a degree as possible, go into the pockets of the man who raised that product from the soil. So long as the farmer leaves cooperative activities with their profit sharing to the city man of business, so long will the foundations of wealth be undermined and the comforts of enlightenment be impossible in the country community.

The present condition of living cannot be accepted as satisfactory. There are too many who do not prosper enough, and of the few who prosper greatly, there are certainly some whose prosperity does not mean welfare for the country. Rational progressives, no matter how radical, are well aware that nothing the government can do will make some men prosper, and we heartily approve the prosperity, no matter how great of any man, if it comes because of his rendering service to the community. But we wish, so to shape condition, that a greater number of the small men in business, the decent, respectable, industrious and energetic men, who conduct small businesses, who are retail traders, who run small stores and shops, shall be able to succeed and so that the big man who is dishonest, shall not be allowed to succeed at all. Our aim is to control business, not to strangle it. And above all, not to continue the policy of make-believe strangle toward big concerns that do evil and constant menace towards both big and little concerns that do well. Our aim is to promote prosperity and then to see that prosperity is passed around. But there is a proper division of prosperity. We wish to control big business among other reasons so that we may secure good wages for the wageworker as well as reasonable prices for the consumer. We will not submit to the prosperity that is obtained by lowering the wages of working men and charging an excessive price to the consumer. Nor to that other kind of prosperity that is obtained by swindling investors or by getting unfair advantage over smaller business rivals.